Zoom in on the
LIBERTY BELL

Zoom in on American Symbols

Therese M. Shea

Enslow Publishing
101 W. 23rd Street
Suite 240
New York, NY 10011
USA

enslow.com

WORDS TO KNOW

charter A piece of writing by a government that gives rights to a group.

civil rights The rights that should protect every person's freedom.

colonist A person who lives in a new country.

inhabitant A person who lives in a certain place.

inspire To make someone want to do something.

proclaim To announce loudly.

protested Showed or expressed strong disagreement with something.

steeple A tall, pointed tower.

symbol An object that stands for something else.

CONTENTS

A Special Bell

The Liberty Bell is a famous symbol of freedom in the United States. The bell first became linked to the idea of liberty, or freedom, because of the special words on it: "Proclaim Liberty throughout all the Land unto all the Inhabitants thereof."

These words and the bell's ringing were meant to remind people of their freedom. Both have inspired those who wanted more rights during different times in American history. The bell even played a part in forming the United States.

The writing on the Liberty Bell came to stand for many kinds of freedom for different groups of Americans.

Close Up

The Liberty Bell weighs 2,080 pounds (943 kilograms). It is made of bronze. The mixture of metals contains copper, tin, and small amounts of lead, gold, arsenic, silver, and zinc. The bell's wooden mount is made of American elm.

The Bell's Beginning

The bell was ordered from England in 1751. That year marked fifty years since Pennsylvania founder William Penn created a charter that gave colonists many freedoms. The ringing of the bell was meant to honor the charter.

Words on the bell tell who ordered it and for what place: "By Order of the Assembly of the Province of Pensylvania for the State House in Philad."

In the days when the Liberty Bell was made, people spelled words in different ways. Pennsylvania is spelled "Pensylvania" on the bell. "Philad" is short for "Philadelphia."

The assembly, the Pennsylvania lawmakers, needed a bell to call their members to the state house for meetings. A bell was also a way to gather colonists to hear news.

Getting It Right

The first time the new bell, called the State House Bell, was rung, it cracked. This is not the crack we see today, though. The bell was melted down and the metal was used to make a new bell. This time, the bell did not sound right. It was melted down and made yet again.

The bell rang from the steeple of the Pennsylvania State House.

The lawmakers did not like the sound of the third bell either. They ordered a new one from England. When the British bell was rung, they did not think it sounded any better. The assembly decided to keep the State House Bell in the Pennsylvania State House steeple to call them together.

Ringing in History

The State House Bell played a part in the birth of the United States. There are many important events when it is said to have been rung. Many people think it was rung to call the assembly to meetings about British taxes on the colonies in the 1760s. These taxes were one reason the colonists later fought for independence. It may have also been rung to

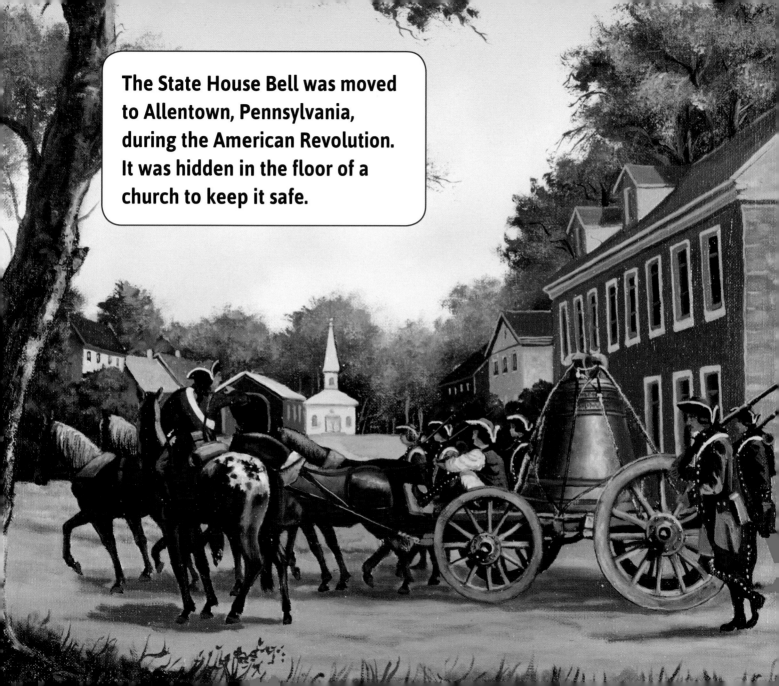

announce the battles at Lexington and Concord in 1775, the first of the American Revolution.

The bell was taken out of the steeple in 1777. The colonists were worried that the British would melt it down and use the metal to make cannons. The bell was hidden, but returned to the state house the next year.

No one knows for sure how the bell got its

Did It Ring?

A story in 1847 called "Ring, Grandfather, Ring" made the bell even more famous—for something that never happened. In the story, the bell was rung on July 4, 1776, to mark the signing of the Declaration of Independence. Many think the bell was rung on July 8, 1776, to call people to hear the Declaration of Independence for the first time. Some historians now think this is untrue, too.

Metal was removed from both sides of the crack so the sides would not rub. Then rivets, or short rods, were placed in the crack.

famous crack. Most believe it cracked in 1835 while ringing for the funeral of John Marshall, the Chief Justice of the US Supreme Court. However, the wide crack you see today is actually a repair!

In 1846, the city of Philadelphia wanted the bell to ring for George Washington's birthday. Metal workers drilled into the thin crack, making it wider and less likely to spread. But another crack began, beginning from the abbreviation for Philadelphia and running up through the word "Liberty." The bell was never rung again.

Symbol for So Many

The State House Bell was first called the "Liberty Bell" or "Bell of Liberty" in 1835 by abolitionists. These people wanted to abolish, or do away with, slavery. The bell was a symbol for their movement. For them, the words on it meant that all people who lived in the United States should have their liberty.

After slavery ended following the American Civil War (1861–1865), the Liberty Bell was taken across the country

for Americans to see. It was presented as a symbol of American freedom and a country united once again.

Women's Liberty

"Liberty" means "freedom," but also "a right." The women's rights movement of the early 1900s fought for women to have the same

An abolitionist poem called "The Liberty Bell" appeared in anti-slavery newspapers, further spreading the name.

Tapped for Victory

The Liberty Bell does not ring anymore. Sometimes it is tapped, though. During World War II, it was tapped for radio listeners on June 6, 1944, to mark the Normandy Invasion. This event led to France's freedom from enemy forces and later the end of the war.

rights as men. They used the Liberty Bell as a symbol for their fight for the right to vote.

A copy of the bell was made in 1915. It was chained so that it could not ring until women were given the right to vote. In 1920, they finally received that right. The bell was taken to the state house, now called Independence Hall, and rung in celebration.

Groups hoping to win certain rights still use the Liberty Bell as a symbol for their fight, just as the women's rights movement did.

The Civil Rights Movement

In the 1960s, African Americans protested at the Liberty Bell in Independence Hall. The group hoped people would realize that the freedoms the bell symbolized were not enjoyed by all US citizens. This was a time when blacks were asking for their civil rights to be protected by the government. Later, laws were passed to provide civil rights for African Americans.

The Liberty Bell is tapped gently each year on Martin Luther King Day to honor the famous civil rights leader and the civil rights movement.

Protesting African Americans are pictured around the famous symbol of American freedom.

Still Inspiring

On January 1, 1976, the Liberty Bell was moved to a building near Independence Hall for a celebration of the nation's founding. In 2003, it was placed in a new building called Liberty Bell Center, which is part of Independence National Historic Park. The bell is now surrounded by glass, and Independence Hall can be seen beyond it.

About two million people visit the Liberty Bell each year. They want to see the symbol that has inspired people in the

Each Fourth of July, the Liberty Bell is tapped thirteen times to remember the thirteen colonies that fought for the liberty of the United States.

past to fight for the rights that we all enjoy today. Even though it rings no longer, the Liberty Bell will continue to call people to fight for freedom and equality.

1. Draw an outline of a bell for each group of people inspired by the Liberty Bell. Use the outline on the next page to help you.

2. On the mount of the bell, write the name of the group (for example, women's rights movement).

3. Do research at the library or online to find out when and how each group achieved their goals.

4. Write what you learn in the body of the bell. (For example, the Voting Rights Act of 1965 outlawed practices that stopped African Americans from voting.) There may be more than one answer in each bell.

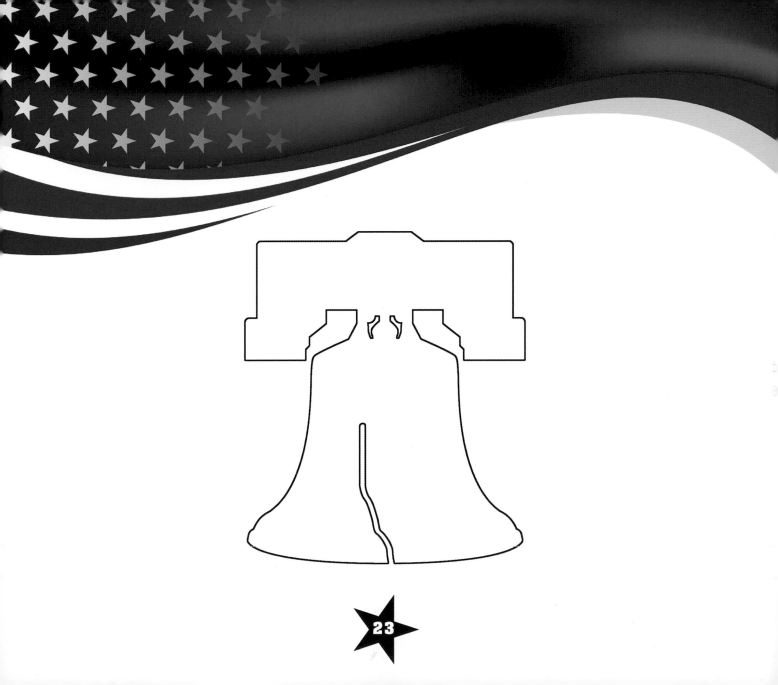

23

LEARN MORE

Books

Francis, James. *Visit the Liberty Bell.* New York: Gareth Stevens Publishing, 2012.

Gaspar, Joe. *The Liberty Bell.* New York: PowerKids Press, 2014.

Marcovitz, Hal. *Liberty Bell: Let Freedom Ring.* Philadelphia: Mason Crest, 2015.

Websites

National Park Service
www.nps.gov/inde/index.htm
Learn about the Liberty Bell as well as Independence Hall.

USHistory.org
www.ushistory.org/libertybell/
Discover more historical facts about the famous bell.

INDEX

Published in 2017 by Enslow Publishing, LLC.
101 W. 23rd Street, Suite 240, New York, NY 10011

Copyright © 2017 by Enslow Publishing, LLC.

All rights reserved.

No part of this book may be reproduced by any means without the written permission of the publisher.

Cataloging-in-Publication Data
Names: Shea, Therese.
Title: Zoom in on the Liberty Bell / Therese M. Shea.
Description: New York : Enslow Publishing, 2017 | Series: Zoom in on American symbols | Includes bibliographical references and index.
Identifiers: ISBN 9780766084544 (pbk.) | ISBN 9780766084568 (library bound) | ISBN 9780766084551 (6 pack)
Subjects: LCSH: Liberty Bell—Juvenile literature. | Philadelphia (Pa.)—Buildings, structures, etc.—Juvenile literature.
Classification: LCC F158.8.I3 S44 2017 | DDC 974.8'11—dc23

Printed in the China

To Our Readers: We have done our best to make sure all website addresses in this book were active and appropriate when we went to press. However, the author and the publisher have no control over and assume no liability for the material available on those websites or on any websites they may link to. Any comments or suggestions can be sent by e-mail to customerservice@enslow.com.

Photos Credits: Cover, p. 1 (inset) Songquan Deng/Shutterstock.com; cover, p. 1 (background flag) Stillfx/Shutterstock.com; p. 5 Atomazul/Shutterstock.com; p. 7 Chris Howey/Shutterstock.com; p. 8 Alison Hancock/Shutterstock.com; p. 11 SuperStock/Getty Images; p. 13 Rebekah McBride/Shutterstock.com; p. 15 The Liberty Bell by Friends of Freedom, Boston, 1856. Anti-Slavery Society 1839-1858. Jon A. Lindseth Suffrage Collection. Courtesy of the Division of Rare and Manuscript Collections, Cornell University Library; p. 17 Buyenlarge/Archive Photos/Getty Images; p. 19 © AP Images; p. 21 Jupiterimages/Photos.com/Thinkstock; interior pages graphic elements amtitus/DigitalVision Vectors/Getty Images (flag page borders), funnybank/DigitalVision Vectors/Getty Images (flag in circle).